Sometimes people do the most eccentric things.

Whatever moved Dorothy to go on loving an un-faithful husband? What prompted Dana and Gwen to give up their Spanish dream house in Santa Barbara? What insane notion caused Marion to turn her back on the one man who truly loved her? What made Dave leave the security of a good job to strike out on his own? Why did C.T. leave honor and riches to go to the jungles of the Congo?

Interestingly enough, all of them did what they did for the same reason. And all of them came out the better for having done it.

As you read these stories, you'll discover a little-known secret of living abundantly by giving away.

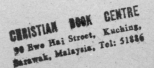

PAT BROOK'S

CLIMB MOUNT MORIAH

Whitaker House

© 1974 by Whitaker House
Printed in the United States of America
International Standard Book Number:
0-88368-024-6

Whitaker House
504 Laurel Drive
Monroeville, Pennsylvania 15146

*All Scripture passages in this book are quoted from the
New American Standard Bible (NASB), and are used by
permission.*

Is it hard for you to understand why certain things have happened to you? You are not alone. Here is a series of true stories about the real conflicts of real people—people who cried out "Why," and then discovered the answer.

The whole book revolves around a simple law that has been proved in the laboratory of personal experience time after time: that God gives His best to those who are willing to yield their best to Him.

Be prepared, then, to look back four thousand years behind the flap of a tent, and see an old nomad who took this principle seriously, submitted himself to the acid test, and came out of the experience rejoicing.

Be prepared, also, to read the intriguing stories of twentieth century people who have dared to try the same principle, and have been delighted with the results.

Above all, do not try to quiet the still, small voice of God who deals with you as you read. This is a strong book, not for the cowardly, but for those who want truthful answers to some of life's most mystifying questions.

CONTENTS

Part 1

ABRAHAM

CHAPTER ONE

A PROMISE FULFILLED

The hungry baby turned his face toward the tickly, warm thing that touched his cheek, his mouth wide open like a baby bird's. Suddenly he had a mouthful of white beard, and let out an infuriated yell. Rooting a few more times in vain, little Isaac slithered in the ancient arms of his father.

Abraham was terrified. Could such a tiny baby leap out of his arms? Tiptoeing stiffly toward Sarah's bed, the patriarch held the squirming baby in his gnarled hands. Wistfully, he watched the casual expertise of his wife, as she took her tiny son deftly in one arm, quieting him in a moment.

Sarah still had the earmarks of an earlier

beauty as she sat up in bed, nursing her newborn child. A smile played about her face, adding to the new radiance Isaac's birth had brought her, as his tiny fist wrapped around her thumb and clutched it tightly.

But then she thought of her ninety years of barrenness when God's promise of a son had seemed like an idle tale. She remembered laughing just twelve short months ago when God promised her and Abraham this son within the year. She knew nothing was impossible with God, in an intellectual way. Why had it been so hard to *believe* the God who had called them out of their old life into a completely new one?

Worse yet had been her attempt to "help God" keep His promise by allowing her young slave girl, Hagar, to sleep with her husband for a night. She knew it was wrong, but she wanted so badly to give Abraham a child! She winced as she recalled her failure to trust God for His way. After Ishmael was born, she hated what she had done.

Oh well, no matter, now. The aching void was filled with the promised child. Isaac means "laughter." Now joy and laughter filled this home! Swept away in a flood of happiness were the memories of thousands of childless yesterdays. The tedious years of waiting for him seemed like a forgotten dream, as she cuddled her little son.

Abraham slipped out of the tent, reliving that

night when the word of the Lord had come to him in a vision. God had said, "Look toward the heavens, and count the stars, if you are able to count them. . . . So shall your descendants be." [1]

Abraham remembered wondering who could count the stars. How could he ever have a son whose descendants would be as many as the heavenly bodies above his head?

Abraham smiled, gazing up at the star-studded sky. Yes, the Lord could be trusted to keep His word; a lusty infant cry from the tent was abundant evidence of that!

Still, it was almost bewildering to be part of a miracle. As much as the patriarch knew that God could do the impossible, it was still hard to absorb the fact that God had done it for *him*.

It was then that Abraham realized that this child would make a considerable difference in his casual friendships with his pagan neighbors. There'd be a lot of questions to answer, but how could he explain this miracle-baby without explaining the God who gave him? In the natural, there was no explanation for this baby born to a ninety-year-old mother, barren all her life, apart from a miracle of God. Abraham wondered what his neighbors would say when they heard his witness. Would they begin to believe in his God, or reject Him and His servant?

[1] Genesis 15:5

Since a miracle could not be hidden, Abraham saw a new life of testimony stretching out before him. The birth of little Isaac had placed a great responsibility upon him to share the story of his coming with whoever would listen.

He remembered how God had said to him, "I will make you a great nation, and I will bless you, and make your name great; and so you shall be a blessing; and I will bless those who bless you, and the one who curses you I will curse. And in you all the families of the earth shall be blessed." [2]

Abraham mused about why anyone would bother to bless or curse him—unless they understood about his God, and the miracle of Isaac.

Suddenly, he saw it all clearly. The skinny old shoulders straightened up, and there was fire in those eyes beneath the shaggy white brows, as he lifted his face toward heaven. He would tell this news himself. No job for a runner, this. A miracle can make a missionary.

The news spread like fire at the end of the dry season. Abraham and Sarah had their own child! Friends far and near learned of Isaac with amusement and surprise.

By the time the weaning feast was held, many came from far places to see the miracle-child for themselves.

[2] Genesis 12:2,3.

In the early dawn curious goats looked down on the nomadic camp from a purple hillside. They blinked in sleepy surprise at so much activity this early in the day.

Every servant of the patriarch hustled in urgency to get ready for the invasion of guests. The choicest lambs must be butchered, and fires built for the roasting. The grain must be pounded, and the spices prepared. The bakers must measure the flour, and knead in the leaven.

Soon a steady stream of girls with jugs on their heads came and went from the well. There was a sound of singing, starting with the crew who fed the camels, and soon taken up by the water girls. The butcher and his helpers joined in, and the bakers too.

Sarah had been up for an hour or more, giving instructions to the slave girls and checking on the details of the feast. Abraham went into the tent and checked on the little sleepy-head, Isaac, who was just beginning to stir. The chubby little fellow rubbed his eyes, blinked a couple of times, and then gave a toothy smile to his old father. Gathering him up and swinging him onto his shoulders, Abraham carried him to the patient nurse, who had been waiting for nearly an hour to dress him.

Soon the nurse busily followed the toddler, as he wandered from group to group in the busy compound, looking up into familiar faces. He wondered, *Why are they all so excited? Why are they making such a fuss over me?*

A cook stooped and gave him the most tender morsel from a skewer. The water girls put down their jugs and curtsied to him, giggling merrily. His father's chief steward grabbed him, scooping him up into his arms with pride that he could take such liberties. As the sun climbed higher in the sky, all was laughter. Isaac was here!

Sarah's heart leaped for joy as she saw her son swung down by the steward, right in the center of the ceaseless activity. Her face flushed with happiness as she watched Isaac go from servant to servant, looking up with a special smile for each one. What a prince he was, her Isaac!

Soon the guests began to arrive; the nearer ones on foot, the distant ones by camel train. Before long a hubbub of excited voices could be heard everywhere on the compound. Sounds of reunion mingled with gales of laughter as ancient family jokes were shared. Everyone was eager to meet the young heir and present their gifts.

By noon the guests were seated beneath the tamarisk trees for the sumptuous feast. All the servants and their children were called upon to serve. All, that is, but one.

A lone, sullen youth stood unnoticed in the shadow of the great tent. He watched the flurry of attention around the two-year-old Isaac with murderous hate. Clenching his fists many times on his staff, he longed to do away with that young life which had put his own into oblivion.

No feast for me, he thought, *even though I'm his son, too. They're ashamed of me, Ishmael, the bastard, reminder of their folly. Now that they have a son of their own, they pretend I never was, like a dried-up water hole after a sandstorm. But I have rights—the rights of the firstborn!*

The young man's face contorted as his jealousy consumed him. Watching another group of guests bowing before his father and the young heir, Ishmael's eyes narrowed and his lips turned downward in scorn. Then he bowed himself, in mock obeisance, only to have his eyes meet with the dreaded Sarah's as he drew himself up.

She stood not five feet from him, just inside the door of the tent. Her eyes shot forth sparks of fury as an iron purpose formed in her soul.

Ishmael blanched in fear as she stepped toward him, saying nothing, but motioning for him to follow her. She made her way back to Abraham without speaking to any of the guests who called to her as she passed.

When she reached her husband, she ignored his jovial greeting. Leaning over, she began to whisper rapidly in his ear, pointing to the frightened teenager behind her.

The patriarch's face reddened, and he shook his

head in vigorous disagreement. But it was no use. Sarah put her hands on her hips, nodding rapidly toward Hagar who was serving nearby, her lips pressed tight together in a thin line. She ignored the men who ate with her husband and son as she left them with her final word:

"Drive out this maid and her son, for the son of this maid shall not be an heir with my son Isaac." [8]

Abraham's face flushed hotly at the open rebuke of his wife in front of his friends. How dare she talk to him like that! Usually she called him "Lord," and he could never remember her resistance of his authority before.

The rest of the afternoon was torture for Abraham. He hardly knew what was going on around him as he tried to smile and nod in response to small talk. The father's heart within him wrenched as he watched Ishmael join in games with other adolescents, while the talk around him centered only on Isaac. Yet every upward look of the trusting face of the two-year-old made his anguish worse: was the child really safe growing up near his jealous half-brother?

Somehow Abraham managed to get through the afternoon. He heaved a great sigh as the last camel train was seen off in late afternoon.

In the twilight he walked far from the compound, up the hillside where his goats and sheep

[8] Genesis 21:10

were grazing. Now he faced the only One Who knew the answer to the dilemma of what to do about the son born of his sin. Having made an irrevocable mistake in the past, how could he now redeem the situation within the will of God?

The Almighty always hears the desperate prayer of one who is prepared to pay the cost of its answer. He answered His servant, not with the words Abraham wanted to hear, but those he *needed* to hear: "Do not be distressed because of the lad and your maid; whatever Sarah tells you, listen to her, for through Isaac your descendants shall be named. And of the son of the maid I will make a nation also, because he is your descendant." [4]

The old shoulders stooped; the bearded chin dropped down on the weary chest. In the quiet of that moment Abraham knew there was only one thing to do. He must obey.

"So Abraham rose early in the morning, and took bread and a skin of water, and gave them to Hagar, putting them on her shoulder, and gave her the boy, and sent her away. . . ." [5]

A hard thing? Yes, but not nearly so hard as trying to live with the results of disobedience.

And there were hidden blessings—like learning obedience that would prepare him for the Big Climb of his life, still two decades away.

[4] Genesis 21:12,13
[5] Genesis 21:14

CHAPTER TWO

THE GREAT TESTING

"Abraham!" God called.

Immediately recognizing the familiar voice, Abraham stopped dead and replied eagerly, "Here I am!" [1] He stood there with head lifted toward heaven, sure he was about to hear some special word about his beloved son. Isaac's years of growing up had been quiet ones as far as hearing from God was concerned, but Abraham had waited patiently.

But what God said almost turned Abraham to cold stone: "Take now your son, your only son, whom you love . . . and go to the land of Moriah; and offer him there as a burnt offering on one

[1] Genesis 22:1

25

of the mountains. . . ." [2] He felt the shock of the searing words traveling up and down his spine. Weakness enveloped him, turning his knees to water. His eyes blurred and his head felt faint, as he leaned hard upon his staff to support the seeming extra weight of his body.

Great beads of perspiration shone on his forehead. His damp hands shook so hard that he lost his grip on the staff and stumbled to his knees.

Perhaps I heard wrong, he thought, pushing himself up slowly. *I must have missed my guidance. How could God ever ask a thing like that? Human sacrifice? That's the way of the heathen. They burn their children to their gods, but that's not the way of my God of love.*

Kill Isaac? Unthinkable. How could this be God? Why, all His promises rest on Isaac. No Isaac, no family. No family, no multitude of descendants like the stars above. It must be a terrible mistake.

Yet that voice. I know God's voice. He called me out of Ur of the Chaldees, and then out of Haran, to this place. He promised me a son, and gave him to me. He promised me this land for our descendants.

Reeling, the patriarch leaned over unsteadily to pick up his staff again. Wobbling toward his tent,

[2] Genesis 22:2

even more unwelcome thoughts forced their way into his mind.

But God did tell me to send Ishmael away, didn't He? His way is not always easy. And I do know that voice.

But what if I were to disobey? Would He hear me when I called to Him after that? Would He leave me at the mercy of my enemies? Would He still bless my fields and flocks as He always has? Can I risk rebellion toward Him?

What? Be counted as His enemy when He has been my Friend? Try to continue life without His presence? Never! Even death would be better than that!

"So Abraham rose early in the morning and saddled his donkey, and took two of his young men with him and Isaac his son; and he split wood for the burnt offering, and arose and went to the place of which God had told him." [3]

The old man's bones drove down deeper into the saddle with every shift of the donkey's back. The animal's gait was unbearably slow. Isaac and the young men were often out of sight, as they walked ahead on the winding path.

It had been a three-day journey. Now they were in the foothills of the land of Moriah. For a long time Abraham had ridden in abject silence, his

[3] Genesis 22:3

sorrow too deep for words. Now his chin rested on his chest, his eyes shut. The donkey would continue to plod the path. No need to look ahead. The heartbroken father would see the dread hill soon enough.

Suddenly the donkey stopped, balking as if something obstructed his path. Abraham opened his eyes. Muttering irritably, he dug his heels into the donkey's sides. Still the stubborn animal refused to move. Then Abraham looked up. There it was in the distance: the hill God had described to him. No heavy forest in that bleak place. Just scrub timber, carelessly strewn on the hillside with the rocks. The early morning haze, coupled with the blowing sand, shrouded most of the slope. Only the barren, foreboding crest could be seen. Abraham shuddered as he thought of the other side of that summit, where God had told him he must build the altar.

So intent was the old man on staring at his destined meeting place with God that he was oblivious to the servants who stood respectfully with Isaac waiting for instructions. They must have been somewhat surprised when Abraham said to them, "Stay here with the donkey, and I and the lad will go yonder; and we will worship and return to you." They watched in silence as Abraham lifted the bundle of wood and laid it on

28

Isaac's back, then took the firepot and knife, and walked away with Isaac.

Did Isaac know he carried the means of his own destruction on his back, as he trudged on in silence, obedient to his father?

Or did the anguished father admit to his son that he brought the fire and knife in his hands to kill him? No, not even when Isaac asked that inevitable question, "Behold, the fire and the wood, but where is the lamb for the burnt offering?"

Abraham answered simply and matter-of-factly, "God will provide for Himself the lamb for the burnt offering, my son." [4]

They walked on together, and Isaac asked no more questions.

As they reached the summit, stinging gusts buffeted them. Leaning into the moaning wind, the patriarch made his way across the barren knob, motioning for Isaac to follow him. Slowly, painfully, he crept toward the far side of the crest. Even the swirling sand, nearly blinding his weeping eyes, could not fully hide that vividly familiar spot ahead which had haunted his mind's eye for three long days.

"Then they came to the place of which God had told him; and Abraham built the altar there, and

[4] Genesis 22:7,8

arranged the wood, and bound his son Isaac, and laid him on the altar on top of the wood." [5]

The Spirit of God veils that holy scene with silence more final than a sandstorm or the mountain top which shut out the view to the waiting servants. No human ear but Isaac's has ever heard the agony of his father's revelation.

But this we know: Isaac obeyed. How easily he could have overpowered his aged father and escaped! How rationally he could have thought the old man mad, and left him there.

The drama startles us because Isaac let himself be sacrificed. Surely this mind was in him "which was also in Christ Jesus . . . [who] humbled Himself by becoming obedient to the point of death. . . ." [6] How perfect a type he was of the One Who was to say much later, "I lay down my life, that I may take it again. No one has taken it way from Me, but I lay it down of my own initiative." [7]

Then came the tense moment when Abraham picked up the knife. As Isaac lay there, the plans of a lifetime meant nothing to him. Ambitions and burdens alike were sealed in a tomb marked "past." One stark reality of the present rendered all prior events meaningless: the shining blade in

[5] Genesis 22:9
[6] Philippians 2:5,8
[7] John 10:17,18

his father's upraised hand. Still, a serene calm pervaded that moment; his silent acceptance gave the sacrificial tabloid its mark of divine approval: *peace*.

Not in Abraham, however. The keen-edged dagger in his clenched fist was dull compared to the invisible one which stabbed his father-heart. Like wave upon wave of malarial fever the pain swept through his body, his head, his starkly rigid arm ending in the murderous blade. If only the command could be reversed, the knife plunged through his own spent chest!

But wait! A shaft of light suddenly flashed in the patriarch's mind. Jehovah, the Everliving One, was not a God of death! He who had given Isaac to Sarah in hopeless, aged barrenness, knew no impossibilities. If He intended to keep His promise of making Isaac into a nation, then He would surely raise him from the dead!

Gethsemane prayers plunged through his mind as shameless tears fell onto the hoary beard. One great sigh and the issue was resolved: *Not my will but thine be done*.

No longer shaking, the hand holding the dagger tensed for its powerful descent.

Suddenly a voice thundered from heaven.

"Abraham, Abraham!"

One earth-stopping cry. Beads of sweat on Abra-

31

ham's brow. Dagger poised in mid-air. A hoarse whisper: "Here I am." [8]

God said to him, "Do not stretch out your hand against the lad, and do nothing to him; for now I know that you fear God, since you have not withheld your son, your only son, from Me." [9]

The old arm trembled, falling lifeless at the father's side as the knife slipped unnoticed to the ground. A dead man dropped that blade. One died there on that mountain, but not Isaac. The proud father, ambitious for and possessive of his beloved son and heir, died to all his personal desires, choosing instead to become alive to the will of God. Gone were Abraham's plans and schemes to make Isaac richer in this world's goods. Gone were daydreams of his pagan neighbors' esteem heaped on Isaac. *Gone was the idolatry of his heart.*

Just then he heard a commotion behind him and the bleating of a sheep. Turning quickly, he saw a ram caught in the thicket by its horns.

Quickly grabbing up his knife, he cut Isaac loose. Together, they caught the ram and offered it to God. And Abraham named the place Jehovah-jireh: "The Lord will provide."

Father and son embraced each other as they watched the dying embers of the substitute sacri-

8 Genesis 22:11
9 Genesis 22:12

fice. They knew now that God could be trusted to keep His Word. What love filled their hearts for the One Who had loosed Isaac from the cruel bonds of death!

Did these men suspect that they had just fore-shadowed earth's greatest drama, the pivotal point of history? Did the patriarch know that God also had an only Son? Did Abraham realize that the only way the life of the human race could be spared was for God to send that Son to die?

Probably not. But he *believed* the living Word Who had called to him from heaven. And Abraham's faith was accepted by the Lord even though he did not understand that God's Son was "the Lamb . . . who takes away the sin of the world." [10] But by the substitionary sacrifice of the ram, God had taught His servant an important lesson—one each of us must learn if we are to be His children: "Without shedding of blood there is no forgiveness."

In calling the place "Jehovah-jireh," Abraham had learned much more of God's character. The God who always lives is the God who always gives. No mount He calls His people to climb is ever higher than the timberline of His grace. In the bleakest human moment there is always a thicket nearby, with God's provision in it.

Then the angel of the Lord called to Abraham a

[10] John 1:29

second time, and said, "By Myself I have sworn, . . . because you have done this thing, and have not withheld your son, your only son, indeed I will greatly bless you, and I will greatly multiply your seed as the stars of the heavens, and as the sand which is on the seashore; and your seed shall possess the gate of their enemies. And in your seed all the nations of the earth shall be blessed, because you have obeyed My voice." [11]

Abraham wept, hearing these surprising words, as he and Isaac prepared to return to their camp. Now he knew that God's word of command was never His *final* word; for the obedient, His words of blessing always follow. Since Abraham *withheld nothing* from God, he was to find that God would now withhold no good thing from him or his descendants.

The wind storm had spent its fury as father and son made their way down the rocky path from Mount Moriah. No burdens now! For both, the ordeal was forever behind them. Isaac wondered what it meant "to possess the gate of his enemies" as his sandaled feet carried him swiftly back to the world of people. His strong shoulders thrilled to God's promise as he began his swift descent. Ahead lay a new life of mastery over every evil which might array itself against him!

For Abraham, the inner burden had been lifted,

[11] Genesis 22:15-18

and now there was a great peace. The aged face reflected the inner calm of one who had squandered all upon the faithful God, only to find himself the richer, having lost nothing.

Down, down they went—down to the two young men, to share the account of God's mercy.

Back now—back to Beersheba, the place of wells. There, people would see how God could bless those who dared to obey Him in all things.

> God of Abraham,
> Spare me no mountain
> Which stands between us.
> Draw me to the summit
> Of your earthly purpose for me.
> May my will be one with Yours,
> Fast closed upon the knife of death
> To every earthly love
> Which means too much.
> Shorn of all idols,
> May my heart be liberated
> In the new song of victory:
> "Jesus is Lord!"
> God of Isaac,
> Spare me no altar
> Where self-life can die.
> "Bind the sacrifice with cords,
> Even unto the horns of the altar."
> Raise high the dagger of Your Word
> To all ambition, plans of my own.

Slain all my scheming,
May new life be resurrected
In union with Yours,
Jesus, my Lord.

Part 2

IN ABRAHAM'S WAY

CHAPTER THREE

THE MARITAL MOUNTAIN

We who live in the far north country have a *fact* of life which is always with us, and which governs many of our daily decisions. Even when daffodils and tulips line our walks, we are never really able to forget the *fact* which determines how deep they are planted.

After the *fact*, watching the boats which dot our lakes and rivers, we forget that only a few brave souls dare to brave the waterways at other times. The *fact* makes ice-fishing a way of life for hardy souls who must get out anyway, and who consider the bitter winds a challenge. But their fur hats and zippered weather gear show that they cannot ignore the *fact*, or live without reference to it. Indeed, the brisk trade in the ski shops and the amount spent on insulated togs is mute testimony to the inescapable *fact* which causes their need. That *fact* is winter.

No one would guess that such a *winter-fact* has ever marred the contentment of a happily married, outstanding couple like the Brownings. For thirty years they have lived together in the perennial springtime of a deep love for each other. Dorothy still puts on stockings every day, and changes her dress before Jack gets home for dinner—even when their married daughter and college son are home and kid her about it. It is a way of life for Dorothy to pray for Jack many times each day as she works about the house. He knows that her encouragement and prayers have brought about his recent promotion in the company where he works.

To the casual observer of this marriage, the Brownings' life often brings reactions of wistful longing. In an age when the shadows of divorce hang over one wedding out of every three, Jack and Dorothy have an aura of sunshine about them which has caused the secret envy of many of their friends. Their pastor has held them up before the rest of the church as a shining example of the scriptural marriage pattern in Ephesians 5. How amazed he and others might be if they knew the winter backdrop which lay behind this marital scene until recently.

In the quiet of their own bedroom, the Brownings had experienced the heartbreak of sexual failure. Despite her deep love for Jack, Dorothy was frigid. Although she was understanding with her husband and glad for his own ability to experience release, the thrill of a normal sex relationship was unknown to her. For his part, Jack spent their early marriage years trying to help Dorothy find fulfillment. However, as the years slipped by and hope faded for anything better, he began to know a gnawing hunger for a more complete union. It cut away at something in his manhood to think that he was unable to arouse his wife to full passion.

Gradually this wholesome desire to captivate his wife began to be replaced by a more general need to experience sex at its fullest: to *know* that he was capable of arousing and satisfying a woman. At first his mind dwelt on this thing fleetingly. Eventually it became an obsession with him, and he found himself staring at the figures and legs of girls in his office. In this state, he found himself prey to a vicious lust which seized him suddenly, without warning, in the presence of attractive women.

An earnest Christian, Jack felt shame and fear at the violence of his sexual feelings. He began to dread being in mixed company and to make all kinds of excuses to avoid social and church functions he knew he should attend. His anti-social tendencies puzzled and worried Dorothy, but she never questioned or argued with him about cancelling out special occasions. She just stayed home with him.

Gradually Jack became subject to fits of depression, sometimes reaching the depths of despair which made even suicide seem a reasonable alternative. At this point in his misery, he heard of oppression from evil spirits and learned of the ministry of deliverance. For the first time in his life, a ray of hope shone on his bitter inner darkness.

One night, the Brownings made the two-hour trip to our Friday night prayer meeting, wondering if they would receive help in the deliverance service afterward. They were delighted with the help they could see that others were getting; yet they seemed to have no reaction in themselves when we gave commands against demonic powers. They went home perplexed and disappointed.

All the next day Jack felt restless and upset. Try as he might, he could not settle down to the Saturday chores he had planned. During those difficult hours, some of us were burdened to pray for him. At the exact time of such intercession, he began to undergo a great release which expressed itself in uncontrollable sobs. Later he wrote us this testimony of that amazing afternoon:

"As I was recalling the meeting, my faith began to reach out in belief that God was going to answer prayer for my problem. The Lord saw my faith, and revealed Himself to me through a tremendous experience.

"Suddenly, joy began to fill my soul. It permeated my whole being until I knew without a doubt that Christ had set me free from the spirit of lust which had bound me for many years."

Later that same day Jack felt he must share the wonderful news of his deliverance with Dorothy. He made a fire in the fireplace as she finished washing the last of the supper dishes; then they sat hand-in-hand on the sofa as they had done so many times before, and he told her the story with some apparent difficulty.

It was hard for Dorothy to understand the vicious, unreasoning lust which he said had gripped him so often in the past, but she praised God with him for his deliverance from it.

"Jack, you know I've always loved you and I always will," she said, as she squeezed his hand. "I didn't know why you were so moody, but I never stopped praying God would solve the problem. When you love someone, you ache to help them. Just knowing you were having such an inner battle and trying to get victory over it makes me love you even more. Why, some men go right ahead and give in to their weaknesses!"

Suddenly Jack stiffened and his face blanched. Slowly he pulled forward, burying his face in his hands.

"Dorothy, I've just got to know whether you will still love me even after you know the worst," he whispered.

"But Darling, I already know the worst, don't I?"

Dorothy could feel her heart pounding furiously, and she began to breathe rapidly and unevenly.

"No, you don't," Jack said deliberately. "I made a bad mistake this past year, and I've got to know if you can forgive me."

"What kind of mistake, Jack?" Dorothy could hear her voice rising, but she couldn't help it. "Is there somebody else—some other woman?"

"No,—at least, not now. There *was* an interlude —a very brief one—with someone else." Jack's eyes were closed now, and the pain of his guilt showed on his face.

"What kind of interlude? A flirtation, or a full-fledged affair?" Dorothy could hear the anger in her voice now. Somehow the voice seemed detached—not hers at all. Surely this could not be happening to them! She and Jack could not be the ones discussing such a thing.

Jack winced, kept his eyes shut, and went on.

"Well, I don't know that you could call it a full-fledged affair, for I only slept with her once—and I never saw her afterward."

"*What? You slept with her?* And then you came home and slept with *me?*" Dorothy's voice was not shrill anymore, but a rasping whisper. "Who is she?"

"A call girl in a Los Angeles hotel." Jack almost spat out the words as if glad to be rid of them—glad to be found out at last.

"Not a *prostitute!* Jack, you've got to be kidding." Dorothy felt faint. Suddenly she wished she could turn the clock back an hour, and change the conversation so it would never include this truth about her darling Jack. Inside, she felt a deep revulsion toward this husband she had nearly worshiped for so many years. Now he seemed a jellyfish of a man, more worthy of her pity than anything else. Even his glorious, liberating experience of the afternoon left her unmoved now. Jack's urgent, pleading voice stopped her reverie at this point.

"No, I'm not kidding, Dorothy, and I'm actually glad that you know. You'll never know what I've been through, trying to fight off the temptation to sin in this way. When I finally gave in and did it, I found out it wasn't anything but disgusting. I've been ashamed of myself ever since. And if I weren't absolutely sure that I'm really free right now, I could never tell you about it. I'd always be afraid it might happen again sometime. I've been living in terror that someday you'd find out and react just the way you are reacting right now."

"What other way did you expect me to react?" Dorothy lashed out at him.

"I don't know. With mercy, I guess, and forgiveness. After all, we *are* Christians, aren't we? And aren't Christians supposed to be forgiving?"

"Yes, I guess I'm supposed to bill and coo because you are not seeing this woman anymore. But what guarantee do I have that you will *always* be free?"

The amazed hurt in Jack's eyes when she said that let Dorothy know that she had gone too far. All of a sudden, the tears came, and she sobbed hysterically. When Jack tried to put his arms around her, she wrenched away from him, and said, "Get away from me, you—you—adulterer!"

At that, Jack stiffened, stood up, and went up to their room. As she heard the door close behind him, Dorothy felt more alone than ever in her lifetime. She had never felt like this before, even when both Jack and John Jr. were away. It seemed that her world had come to an end, and no one was left to share the anguish of watching it burn.

The fire died in the fireplace, except for a few smoldering embers. She knew that before morning they would be dead too—as dead as the love she once had for Jack. Somehow she could not move. The minutes ticked by into hours, and her mind seemed numb.

The hall clock announced that it was midnight, and a chorus she had taught the children began to flit through her mind: "Every promise in the Book is mine. . . ." Just this week she had taught that to her Sunday school class, but somehow none of the promises seemed to be hers anymore.

Suddenly she felt she must share her burdens with someone, or die. Our phone number popped into her mind. Dorothy felt that was strange, for she had so recently met us. But, impulsively, she made her way to the kitchen and called us.

Her long distance call woke me up at ten after twelve. As she spilled out the whole story of Jack's confession, Dorothy started to sob again. It took ten minutes for her to get out the story coherently. When she was through, almost as an afterthought, she mentioned Jack's experience of deliverance from his lifelong torment the previous afternoon.

Dorothy is a gentle, loving Christian. Even though we had just met, I could sense that the bitterness in her voice was unusual for her. After she had finished recounting the story of the whole extraordinary day, she summarized her feelings with chilling but perfect insight.

"So here we are, in the midst of one of life's great ironies. Suddenly Jack knows he is free from the torment that has plagued him for so long, and I don't even care. He's killed all the love I ever had for him."

For about a minute and a half, the telephone company computers were clocking up an expensive silence on her bill. Then it seemed that the Lord gave me a flash of insight.

"Dorothy, God says that it's the truth that sets us free. Facing the truth about himself prepared Jack for the Lord's deliverance; and now that *you* know this truth as well, you too can find a deeper freedom in Jesus. In your concern for Jack over the years, you've been unaware that there are areas in your own life in which *you* need deliverance. That's why God has let you hear the worst, so He can set you free in all those areas."

"Me? Free from what?" Dorothy's voice sounded a little hesitant—even incredulous.

"Well, free from self-righteousness, for a starter. Did you ever realize that the Word teaches that if you refuse to forgive Jack, God *cannot* forgive you?" I let that sink in for a minute, propped up my pillow, turned the light on, and reached for my Bible.

"Oh, I think I can forgive him. The real problem is that I don't think I can ever love him again."

"Why not?"

"Because—because—" Dorothy's voice became

shrill and petulant, as she fought for words to describe the terrible earthquake going on inside. "Well, because he's not the Jack I thought I married, that's all. I could still love him as long as I thought he was struggling against this thing, but somehow it's completely different now that I know he's fallen. Why, somehow, he seems so *weak* to me now."

"Ah, now I think we're getting to the root of the problem. What you're saying is that the fallible human being he really is cannot begin to measure up to the nearly perfect man you've loved all these years."

"Well, I never thought of it that way, but I guess you're right, Pat. But what's wrong with that? Doesn't the Bible teach that we are to reverence our husbands?"

"Yes, Dorothy, it does. But it does not say we are to worship them. There's only one person worthy to be adored, and that is the Lord Himself."

"Well, what do I do now? I've got this awful emptiness inside that I don't think I can bear much longer. What will fill this gap in my life? What will soothe this ache?"

"The Lord himself," I answered softly. "Are you familiar with Genesis twenty-two?"

"Yes, I think so. That's the account of Abraham offering up Isaac, isn't it?"

"Yup, the very one. I want you to go read that story—and not just once. Read it until the light dawns in your spirit, and you are able to see what God is saying to you through that chapter. And don't go to bed until you see it."

"All right, I will!" Dorothy's voice was calm again now. It was a relief to hear the glimmer of hope in her answer.

"Call me again if you want. Better still, plan to come up and see me whenever you can. Let me know what God says to you through that amazing portion of Scripture."

"I will. And thank you for listening."

Monday morning, Dorothy phoned that she'd like to come up, if it was all right with me. It was fine, and she arrived about lunch time. I breathed a sigh of relief as soon as I opened the door and saw her, for she was literally enveloped in the peace of God.

As we sat together over lunch, she poured out this amazing story of how God had met her in the wee hours of the morning, after our phone call.

"I did what you said, Pat; I read that chapter over and over. At first it seemed to make no sense: to have nothing to do with our situation. For one thing, I couldn't even get my mind on the scene in the passage, because of a horrible, imaginary picture of my husband in some grotesque position over some other woman's body.

"I prayed and cried out to God, asking Him to show me some light from this Scripture passage. Then a strange thing happened. Somehow, the picture in my mind's eye changed. I could still see Jack, but this time he was bound with ropes, and lying on a stone altar. I stood there with the knife in my hand, just like Abraham. Suddenly I felt a stabbing pain in my chest, just like the pain I had felt when Jack told me the whole miserable story hours before. I honestly didn't think I'd live through it."

Dorothy paused a moment here. She looked down at her hands folded in her lap, while I waited in silence.

"It was at this point in my life that Christ became the *One* to me. His presence was so real! He reminded me of his unfailing love for me, and of his watchful care over me.

"Deep down inside, I felt that if I would keep my eyes on Jesus, and not fail Him at the crisis in my life, it would please Him. This is my one purpose now."

Tears began to trickle down the cheeks of both of us now. Dorothy went on, very softly.

"He met me then, Pat, in the darkest hour of my desperate need. The pain left my chest, and peace settled over me, like the great surge of an incoming tide. For years I have sung the words of that hymn, 'The love of Jesus, what it is, none but His loved ones know.' But I never knew until the other night what it meant. I don't think I've ever loved Him completely before."

"Do you know why, Dorothy?" I asked.

"Well, I think Jack was first in my thinking. I wanted to keep the enemy from winning our home. I had tried to do this by being a loving, devoted, Christian wife. However, this had not been enough to keep Jack true to me. He tried, but failed. Finding this out turned my world upside down. . . ."

"And toppled Jack from the place in your heart that belongs only to God anyway," I interrupted.

"Do you mean I made an *idol* out of him before?" Dorothy asked me incredulously.

"I know it's a hard thing to face, Dorothy, but it's the truth that sets us free."

Dorothy sat silent for several minutes, looking out our sliding glass doors while I cleared the table. The winter view was fascinating, even after months of the white landscape. On a day as clear as this one, we could see the distant hills and woodlands.

"It's hard to believe your deck out back is at second-story level, Pat," Dorothy mused. "The snow seems so close."

"It's the drifting," I answered. "My teenage

sons tell me it's at least seven feet deep right there. Tell me, Dorothy, have you really forgiven Jack?"

She winced. "I don't know. I keep thinking I have, but then I find myself dwelling on what he's done, and the resentment seems to well up all over again."

I got up, wiping the plastic cloth off with a sponge. "Is that the way God has forgiven you for all those years of idolatry? Or does He treat you as though it had never happened?"

"Well, the Bible says, 'As far as the east is from the west, so far hath He put our transgressions from us.' Since the east never meets the west, I guess He counts the whole thing as though it never happened."

"That's right. Thirty years of idolatry have been washed right off the slate. Can't you do the same for *one incident* of adultery?" The words were not kind, but they were necessary. For a minute Dorothy recoiled, turned her head away from me, and concentrated on the snow scene again.

I tried again. "Dorothy, would you want to live up here if spring never came?"

"Goodness, no," she laughed. "It's our only hope, even if it comes later than in other places. That's not a hard one to answer."

"Well then, the other one should be easy to answer, too." I drove the point home. "Without forgiveness, your home will just be one dreary

55

scene of ice and snow, with no springtime in sight. And your life will stay like those trees out back— barren—without fruit or beauty. Do you see that little tree in the midst of that small clearing at the back of the lot? That's a lilac. In two or three more months, we expect to see that thing loaded with blooms, with birds singing out God's great resurrection theme from its branches. We can count on it, because He's promised that as long as the earth remains, He'll send springtime and harvest. His sunshine and warmth will melt this frozen, dreary blanket our yard is entombed in, and there will be new life everywhere."

"But how does that compare to my problem with Jack?" Dorothy asked with a long, deep sigh.

"Because right now your love is buried under a blanket of unforgiveness which is just as real, and just as bitterly cold, as that snow bank. If you forgive Jack, you will set off the hidden signal which will bring springtime into your relationship. You see, there's one great difference between nature's spring and God's love in our relationships. The first is automatic; the second is not. It depends upon our *willingness* to forgive and love for Jesus' sake."

The injured wife sat very still for several minutes, gazing out at the deep drifts. There was another long, deep sigh. "It's true. I've got to forgive him just the way God forgives me—never bringing it up again, never reliving any of it."

"What better time than right now?"

She nodded silently, and we both closed our eyes. "Lord," she prayed, "I forgive Jack just the way You have forgiven me. And I pray that I can love him again, the way You've been loving me: not letting the past stand between us. In Jesus' wonderful name. Amen."

Today the Browning home is a trophy of God's springtime grace. The love nearly overwhelms you as you come in the door and experience the Lord's own warmth and welcome from the host and hostess. However, this love is different from the kind they once knew. This love is the divine *agape* that reaches out and has enough for everyone who comes. There is power in this *agape* to meet the most desperate human needs—and many an aching soul has been led by the Spirit of God to the doors of the Browning home.

However, it would be dishonest to say that the victory was won in a moment. Dorothy has written me of her personal struggle after she went home that winter day:

"The Lord had answered prayer before, and I was counting on His doing it again. I knew that somehow, although the devil had meant to

57

destroy our home, if we would yield all to Christ, He would give us the victory.

"How many times I cried and said, 'Lord, I can't make it.' And each time it seemed like the answer was, 'I know you can't, *but I can.*' And He did! Praise His name."

Recently a girl whom John Jr. is dating came home from college with him for the weekend. Dorothy showed me her "bread and butter note," which is a fitting testimony to the grace of God in this home:

Dear Mrs. Browning,

Thank you so much for this past weekend. It was more than your kindness to me which I shall remember for a long time. It was the love in your whole family, for one another, and for the Lord Jesus.

I am from a broken home, and I have to admit I was cynical about meeting you, because I thought John was 'putting me on' about how great you people are. Honestly, he didn't half do you justice. I guess it would be hard for someone like you to imagine what it's like being brought up where there's no love, but I can tell you it's awful. Thanks for having plenty to give me, while I was there.

Now I can understand why John is such a great guy.

Sincerely,
Sue Brown

CHAPTER FOUR

THE DREAM HOUSE

One of the most beautiful cities in the world is Santa Barbara. There, Old World Spanish charm is blended with contemporary California, and the result is a delight to the senses. Driving into the town on the coastal highway, Dana and Gwen Taylor were struck immediately by the tall, graceful palms, swaying gently in the balmy breeze which whispered gently across the crescent shore-line.

No cloud dared to intrude in the bright azure sky that morning, as the happy couple pulled up to the realtor's office. They were sure they would find their dream home *today*, in this lovely place. For years they had looked forward to settling down and having a home of their own; forgotten now were the years of hardship during college and graduate school. They were almost too happy to talk, as they entered the office and looked for Mrs. Brown's desk.

Cynthia Brown had been contacted by the firm which had just hired Dana, and had arranged to spend this whole Saturday with them. As the young couple approached and introduced themselves, she was struck immediately by an almost electric quality about them. Somehow, there was a special "life" about these people. It was going to be a real treat to find a home for them.

Dana had a handsome pensiveness, with deep, brooding, brown eyes which, at the same time, conveyed a wonderful kindness. Gwen was a beautiful girl with a cameo-like oval face and a serene inner radiance. There was a spiritual quality about both of them that was unusual, as they spoke to the realtor easily about prayer and the Lord's leading them into this step. Wistfully, Cynthia found herself wanting whatever it was they had.

As the three of them drove through one of the charming sections of Santa Barbara, Gwen and Cynthia chatted easily, while Dana was lost in his thoughts. He remembered the hardships of his childhood: the traumatic early years of being orphaned and then adopted by a farmer and his wife; the cold New England winters without indoor plumbing; the chores and many hardships. Most of all, he remembered the loneliness. They lived miles and miles from the nearest boy his age, and the youngest in his adopted family was ten years older than he.

At about the age when Dana learned to drive and could have sought out friends, his father died. This meant he had to help support the family and work every minute when he was not in school, if he was ever to get to college and fulfill his dreams of a professional career. His high school years were filled with long, weary hours of stocking shelves in a supermarket during the days and warehousing at night. After graduation, he took the hardest, most disagreeable jobs the local farmers had, in order to make the most money quickly. He would ride combine (which meant eating dust all day), but he could do it because he was not plagued by the allergies which troubled many of the farmers.

He had hoped his year of hard work after high school would finance his first two years in college, but a knee operation during the spring of that year ate up much of what he had saved. However, instead of despairing, he entered college the following fall as planned, even though he knew his college career would be much like high school had been: work, work, work, and very little else.

The hunger for deep friendships and long discussions with others in his dormitory went unfed during undergraduate years. He had to keep working while the other fellows had their bull sessions and times of propping up feet on desks while they solved the world's problems. Life became a gray business of duty piled upon duty—until he met Gwen.

She was like the spring sunshine after months of dreary winter cloudiness. She listened to him with an appreciation of what he really was, and yearned to share some of his deepest dreams. She understood him, whether he spoke or was silent, and soon they found together that profound love which only comes with oneness.

They were married before his senior year, and had many struggles before his graduate work was finished. But they had been together, and it had all been worth it. During that time, the Lord had brought Dana to a personal knowledge of Himself. Gwen had also become much more deeply committed to Christ, although she had received Him as Savior during her childhood. In recent months, they had prayed together for a home and security, and now the Lord was answering by placing them in this lovely area.

Suddenly Dana realized the car had stopped, for the second time. The first house Cynthia drove by had not appealed to Gwen. Although they had parked in the driveway for a few minutes, Cynthia had simply told the owner that they would not be going through the house. This time, however, Dana was brought out of his reverie by a delighted squeal from Gwen.

As he looked up the hill at the quaint, Spanish-style ranch set back in the trees, Dana put both hands behind his head and gazed at the place, grinning broadly, and letting out a long contented sigh. After they drove up the curved driveway, both bounded out of the car, and almost ran, hand in hand, up the flagstone walk to the front door. Heady scents of roses filled the air, and there was a delightful chorus of birds singing from the trees in the shady part of the lawn.

As they went through the house, both Gwen and Dana felt it was almost too good to be true. There were two bedrooms and two baths, and a lattice-covered patio in the back, where boxed camellias and dwarf lemon trees grew merrily near the house wall. The quaint Spanish ranch was beautifully situated on just the right spot on nearly an acre of land.

The owners, an older couple with no financial problems, were delighted with the Taylors' reaction to their home. They were impressed with Gwen's sparkling radiance and Dana's calm strength, and felt certain the young couple would cherish the place as they had. Apparently they decided "this was it" as surely as the Taylors' did.

They accepted an offer two thousand dollars under their asking price, when the realtor made it clear that the amount was the very maximum the young couple could afford.

Just six weeks later, to the Taylors' amazement and joy, they were at home in this idyllic setting. Every morning Gwen and Dana had their devotions together at the kitchen table in front of the sliding doors by the patio. From the very first, their life in Santa Barbara was one of blessing and joy in countless ways.

A year after their move, little Cindy Taylor was born. She was a real answer to prayer. Gwen had had several miscarriages and lost one baby at full term. Every day when she put Cindy in her carriage out under the trees, she would thank God and sing a chorus or two to their "miracle baby."

Also, within that first year, Dana found deep, lasting friendships which he had longed for all his life. His pastor, Jerry Cochran, was about his age and as hungry for God as Dana himself. Together they prayed, read the Word, and dared to dream of great things that God might do through them. With their wives, they sought God and were met by Him in a mighty way, with the result that all four lives were progressively transformed through their fellowship together.

Out of the igniting that God gave them grew an outreach to the whole community and many other lives were changed. Dana and Gwen held a Bible study for couples in their home, and were over-joyed to see victory after victory for Christ in those that came. The realtor, Cynthia Brown, and her husband found the Lord through these meetings, and they were instrumental in bringing several other couples.

After Cindy was born, Gwen began to have a quiet time with the Lord every day while the baby took her nap. Gwen would kneel beside the redwood chaise on the patio, with her Bible opened before her on the green cushion. Every day she asked the Lord to teach her what He wanted her to learn for that day, and then read three or four chapters of the Word. Then she would pray, and sometimes stay there in the still-ness for ten or fifteen minutes afterward, just wait-ing on God.

One thing troubled Gwen, and this she found very hard to understand. From the time she had moved into this beautiful home, she had felt *guilty* about being there. Often she would think, in vivid terms, of those less fortunate, living in hovels or in the squalor of one or two overcrowded rooms. Why should this be? Was she having some kind of neu-rotic reaction to the blessings God was showering on her and Dana? Had they not prayed for this place, and had not God abundantly answered?

The only way she could reassure herself was to

praise God for their home and say to Him, "I'm glad this is Yours. Thank You for giving it to us, Lord." Nearly every day for two or three months, Gwen ended her time of devotions on that note, and then got up and resumed her chores. But the next morning, the nagging guilt feelings would still be there.

One day, just after Gwen had prayed about everything she could think of, she became distinctly aware of the Lord's Voice speaking down in her spirit.

"Can you give Me this house?"

"No, no!" came the anguished cry from her lips. "Lord, how could You take this away from us?"

There was no answer—only the graceful murmuring of the palms as a fresh ocean breeze flitted its way over the hill. Inside, Gwen felt a terrible churning, like the Santa Barbara waves on a stormy day. All was choppy, and the feeling of peace she had known during her prayer time had vanished as quickly as the bright blue sky during the rainy season.

Morning after morning, in the weeks that followed, Gwen tried to argue with God about this unreasonable request. After all, hadn't Dana needed the security of this home far more than she? Wasn't it just the perfect place to bring up Cindy and lead other people to the Lord? Were they not witnessing in all the avenues of contact with people that God had given them?

There was no further word from the Lord, and there was no peace in Gwen's heart. The burden of guilt became ominous, and the days which had flown by during their first year in Santa Barbara now dragged on interminably. Almost daily, around supper time, Gwen became short tempered with Dana, which baffled both of them.

One morning during her quiet time, Gwen was aware of an overflowing love in her heart for the Lord. Thoughts of His goodness and mercy showered her mind, and an overwhelming sweetness of His presence settled over her. Suddenly she saw the true issue in the turbulent dealings of the past weeks. *Did she really love the Lord Jesus more than her dream home?*

"Yes, Lord, oh yes!" Tears ran down Gwen's lovely face as she answered the unspoken question out loud. In that moment, all the guilt feelings left and she heard the Voice of the Lord for the second time, just as she had weeks before when He had asked her to give up her home.

"You have a little less than two years left here."

Gwen was stunned. God really meant business with her; this was no trial run. He really was going to take away her home! But suddenly it didn't matter anymore, for a marvelous peace had filled her heart, and now there was no stabbing guilt to tear it away.

During the year that followed, the Taylors were happier than they had ever been in their lives. Their home was used of the Lord in ways that amazed them. They started a Tuesday night prayer meeting, and saw many glorious answers to prayer. Many people found the Lord there, and others were filled with the Spirit. Miracles and answers to prayers were regular happenings in those meetings. Dana, Jerry Cochran, and others laid hands on the sick and they were often healed in Jesus' wonderful name.

Then one day it all came to an end. Dana came home one evening, his eyes moist and shining, and told Gwen that the Lord had spoken to him. He was to quit his job as of April first (then six months away), and be prepared to go into the Lord's service full time.

Dana held his fragile little wife close. "It will mean selling the house, Darling, as well as leaving Jerry and Sally and the church. I doubt that God will keep us here in Santa Barbara."

Gwen put her hands on both his cheeks, and looked at him. Dana had never seen her look more radiant. "It's all right, Dear. I settled that one with the Lord over a year ago. He asked me if I could give up this house, and I had no peace until I said 'yes.' I really let the house go that day, and I figure we've just been living here on borrowed time ever since."

Today Dana and Gwen have a youth ministry in a city far from Santa Barbara. The Lord is blessing them and pouring out His Spirit upon the work there in a way that amazes them. Never a week goes by that young people do not find the Savior in their work, and many have been wonderfully delivered from drug addiction and other vise-like bondages.

Dana is quick to give all the glory to God. "It is simply the power of the Holy Spirit," he says. "God wants more than to fill us with His Spirit. He wants us to be directed and guided by Him in even the smallest of details."

Gwen has seen lately that they had to climb Mount Moriah before they could enter this life of blessing.

After hearing me speak on Genesis twenty-two, Gwen said, "My home was *my* Isaac; until I could lay that beautiful place on the altar, and plunge the knife of God's dealings into all my own wishes and plans, I was just plain, ordinary Gwen. Now all that is finished, and He is free to work through me with His power."

"Do you think you'll ever want a home of your own again, Gwen?" I asked her.

"Well, as a matter of fact, we'll soon be moving

into one. It's a colonial bungalow with lots of charm. The thing we like about it is that it'll be maintained easily—aluminum siding and a small yard. The yard will be great for Cindy. Apartment life has been hard on her."

"Tell me more about the place."

"Well, it has two fireplaces—a beautiful one in the living room, and a smaller one in the paneled den in the basement. We expect that this den and the flagstone patio out back will be invaluable for relaxing, both in our very limited leisure and in our times with the young people."

Gwen paused a moment, reflectively, as if weighing the differences between their former experience with the house that had been so hard to give up, and this one, which had now come so easily into their lives. Thoughtfully, she went on.

"Even though there were many things in the first house that we had to sacrifice, it seems as if the Lord has compensated for these. We prayed for one fireplace and got two! We've prayed all along for Cindy's needs to be met in this situation, and it just seems ideal, since there is a playmate next door, and lots of room to play in the long driveway and adjoining yards."

"Where is the house, Gwen?" I asked.

"In the city limits. A nice residential area, but very convenient to downtown. Best of all, I'll be near to many of the friends I've made this year.

The house needs redecorating, but I love doing that kind of thing. When we're finished, we feel it will reflect our personalities.

"I can't wait to move in though. And a real plus in all of this is that this home will cost us less than the other one did, or even our apartment. But the most wonderful asset of all will be that Dana can finally come home to real peace and quiet, as he gets busier and busier in the work. The apartment's been so noisy! It's been a real testing time for us. There's only one night that Dana isn't working, and every weekend lately he's been speaking somewhere. I believe God is giving us back a home now so that it can be a real sanctuary for Dana from the wider and wider ministry God is opening up to him."

"Then your home really *was* your Isaac," I mused. "Not only was it originally given by God and in His will, but you had to give it up, and later you got it back—in a different form."

"Isn't God wonderful!" Gwen exclaimed with that radiant smile of hers. "You never know what He's going to do next!"

CHAPTER FIVE

"I LOVE YOU"

Today we live in an era of revolution. Moral and familial anarchy are a part of this seething, convulsive change in the social order. One marriage out of three ends in divorce in the United States as this book goes to print. This statistic might well be obsolete before a decade has passed.

Christian families are not immune to the diseases of our age which threaten to destroy us. The cancer of a permissive society has spread so far that its end result might well be the title of an English best seller, *The Death of the Family*.

Larry and Marion Carter were a couple typical of many today. In a suburban home in Spokane, they had endured fifteen years of marital misery with bravery "for the sake of the children." They were Christians who read their Bibles, attended church three times a week, tithed their income, and prayed for missions. They sent their children to Christian schools and Bible camps; yet they could not get along with each other.

God used a surprising means to bring them out of their stalemate. His dealings came in a gift-wrapped box labeled "new friends." When the Carters first met the Jarretts, they hit it off immediately. Doing lots of things together, plenty of laughter, and similar interests at church did a lot for both jaded marriages. Then one night, quite suddenly, things changed.

It was during a pot luck supper at church. There was a big crowd present. Because they had come late and few seats were left, the two couples could not sit together. Before she had finished eating, Marion suddenly became aware of Jim Jarrett staring at her from across the room. As she looked up and her eyes met his, it was as if they were alone in that big hall. Nothing else mattered; no one else mattered. Jim's eyes told Marion, "I love you."

Surely she was imagining things, Marion thought. But, no, those eyes said more than any words could ever say. She began to believe that Jim really loved her. The forced smile she had been wearing for years disappeared. In its place, a new sparkle lit up her eyes, and her cheeks flushed like a teenage girl's when she first falls in love.

There were no words exchanged between them after the supper; they carefully avoided one another while jostling for coats and rounding up the children to go home.

Later that night after the children and Larry had gone to bed, Marion took her Bible and slipped down to the kitchen. Sitting at the table, she whispered, "Lord, help me through this temptation. How can I stand being married to Larry now that it looks as though Jim loves me and I can feel myself falling in love with him? Give me a verse to help me."

She opened her Bible and put her finger down on a verse. It was Song of Songs 8:7. "Many waters cannot quench love; neither can the floods drown it." She drew in her breath sharply and started to shake all over. What kind of comfort was this? Where was God when she needed Him so desperately?

Tears began to trickle down Marion's cheeks. She felt them splash onto her hands as she buried her face in them on top of the table. She wept silently for a long time as she thought back over the boredom of her married life.

On their first date, she and Larry had been crowded in the back seat of a car with another couple. She remembered the funny feeling of magnetic attraction toward Larry. Since she had taken this to be some kind of sign that they were "meant for each other," she was easily drawn into a kissing, petting relationship. Before long, Larry was talking about love and begging her to marry him. She did, more from a sense of inevitability than anything else.

Soon the novelty of having all the sex they wanted wore off, at least for Marion. She tried reaching toward him with her mind to establish some basis for companionship, but this failed. They had nothing in common.

At first it seemed like a bad dream. Marion hoped if she brought up enough subjects in conversation, sooner or later she would find one that would interest him. Yet it was all in vain. Larry usually became either hostile or evasive whenever she talked with him.

Gradually it began to dawn on Marion that something was wrong with Larry, terribly wrong. She could get angry with him and even shout at him, but he seemed numb. Occasionally he would shout back, but he never had an appropriate remark to make about their situation. Trying to "talk it out" brought the most discouraging moments of all, however. Larry was a non-communicator.

Larry lived on the surface of things. They had

plenty of food to eat, didn't they? They had a nice home, didn't they? Their sex life was normal, wasn't it? The children were healthy, weren't they?

No matter that her soul cried out for fellowship. No matter that she thought about things that never entered his mind. No matter that she knew a great, gnawing emptiness on the inside, crying out to be filled with companionship.

Time and again she plotted about how best to leave him or divorce him. Time and again her love for her children kept her from making the move.

Then the Lord Jesus Christ came into her life, and the awful emptiness was filled with peace. The Word of God gave her mind the food it had craved. She prayed for things to happen, and they did—even to Larry. He was converted and they had their first thing in common: a relationship with Jesus Christ.

As the years crept by, however, the big changes she had hoped for in her home did not come. Larry was still an emotional cripple. He simply did not react to people or situations the way most people did. Eventually Marion lost interest in her appearance and housework. Resignation replaced the hope of former years, as she tried to get herself into a frame of mind where she could endure life imprisonment. She began to pray that God would make the changes in Larry that would make this possible. Then, seeing little apparent answer to this prayer, she changed her request to, "Lord, make the changes in *me* that are necessary, even if Larry never changes."

Soon after that the Carters met the Jarretts. Now it looked as though she and Jim were falling hopelessly in love.

"Lord, I just don't understand Your way of answering prayer," Marion whispered, as she sat upright again at the kitchen table. She turned the light off and gazed out into the moonlit yard. "Perhaps I'm just being a silly schoolgirl, Lord. Maybe I can forget about Jim by morning and things will be just like they've been before."

Jim called after the school bus left in the morning. Marion soon discovered she had not been imagining things. Could he come over later to drop off some sports equipment Larry wanted? He simply had to talk with her, and could combine the stop with a business call nearby.

That was the beginning. Soon there were surprise phone calls or visits, and meetings at the park for long talks and walks together. It seemed as if the marital silence of a lifetime had vanished for both of them in those happy hours of sharing thoughts and dreams together.

Larry and Esther were never mentioned. They were simply forgotten—part of a hated life too grim to remember. For Marion, facing Larry as he came home from work in the evening became unbearable. She began to think she would scream every time he touched her, and her heart sank as he came into the house each evening.

For a long time Marion and Jim avoided any physical contact except holding hands; but gradually their longing for each other drew them closer together. Soon the long walks included stolen kisses. Marion realized they were heading for real trouble. One day in the park, she and Jim talked frankly about their relationship.

"Why don't we end our respective farces with divorce and get married so that we can have some happiness together?" Jim asked, swinging Marion around to face him on the path.

"Because we're Christians," Marion answered quietly, dropping her eyes beneath his insistent gaze.

"Does God condone hypocrisy?" he asked softly, through clenched teeth.

"No, Jim." Marion was weeping quietly now. "But neither does He condone divorce and immorality."

"Isn't God a God of love?" Jim's face was flushed, with the urgent look of a little boy begging his parents for his first bicycle. "Where does this feeling come from that I have for you anyway? I've never loved anyone the way I love you.

There is no experience in life that I can think of which wouldn't be enriched by your presence."

"And we think so much alike," Marion heard her voice saying. "How wonderful it is to be with someone you can *think* with and *talk* with."

"Exactly!" Jim's face was close to Marion's, his eyes pleading with hers. "This is the oneness marriage is supposed to be—that which the physical is supposed to express."

"And how appalling when it expresses *nothing*." Marion was surprised at the bitterness in her voice, released from behind her carefully guarded mask of many years.

"Just as appalling as the unwelcome advances of someone you cannot love," Jim retorted.

"Or as impossible as the attempt to love someone you cannot respect." Marion finished the thought with a hot splash of fresh tears streaming down her cheeks, as Jim gently cradled her face in his hands.

"Then why go on with it, Darling?" Jim asked huskily, pressing his lips to her bangs as Marion lowered her head in despair.

"Because there's Someone I love even more than I love you, Jim," Marion whispered. "My Lord Jesus."

"I'm afraid I don't feel very good about Him right now, Marion. You say He is a sovereign God. Then why did He bring us together, just to yank us away from each other? He must have known how it would go with us. If He made us, then He must have known we would love each other and want to be together. Why, oh *why*, did it have to happen this way, Darling?" Jim's eyes were moist, and the muscles stood out in his neck as he gripped Marion's elbows and held her at arm's length. His eyes drank in the anguish in hers, and then traveled up to her soft auburn hair and the wide band she wore behind her bangs.

"I don't know, Jim," Marion could hear her voice saying with a strange dullness in it. "We make mistakes, but God never does. Perhaps you and I each made a bad one some time ago. There's no one else we can blame. Nor is there anyone else we can run to, to undo it. The Lord is a specialist in making over broken things. Maybe He had to bring both of us to this point to break us so that He can really make us over."

"Darling, tell me something." There was a dangerous bitterness in Jim's face now, as he lowered his voice. "How can you keep from hating a God who would separate us?"

"You've got it all wrong, my Precious." Her voice whispered to him, as her eyes pleaded with him. "How can you keep from loving Him when He is all you have?" People who have good marriages can never know Him in quite the same way you and I can, for they have some fulfillment *there*,

85

You and I—we have *nothing* apart from Him! And He knows and understands that—even though we must face all kinds of pious advice from other people to 'snap out of it.' He wants to be our all in all, and it's either that or *ruin* for both of us!"

"Then—you're saying—we have no future?" Jim asked, unbelievingly.

Marion stared downward mutely, shuddering slightly through her tears. Her thoughts went back to a passage of Scripture she had read that morning—Genesis twenty-two. Only now, instead of seeing an old man trudging with his young son up Mount Moriah, she saw herself with her beloved Jim. Deep down in her spirit, she was aware of these words: *Will you give him up?*

"Yes," she had whispered, almost inaudibly. The palms of her hands were damp, and suddenly Marion felt very weak. "No matter how much it hurts, I'm going on with Larry somehow—for Jesus' sake."

Once the words were said, the decision final, Marion felt strangely at peace. Oh yes, it hurt terribly to look up at Jim's dear face, twisted in anguish like her own. But suddenly she was aware that they were not alone. *Someone* stood there on the wooded path with them, unheard and unseen, but more real than they were. A sense of His presence brought back the color to her cheeks and the will to go on. Immediately, her dull eyes came ablaze with sparkling light, much like that first night at church when she and Jim realized they loved each other.

Jim had never seen such fire in Marion's face, nor ever loved her more. His own face softened, and his voice became gentle and wondering as his hands slipped down her arms to hold her hands in his. "I've got to admit, God's seemed a lot more real to me since I've known you. There's a look on your face sometimes that opens up heaven for me, and makes me want to know Him better."

"Oh Darling, this is what I've been praying for. Somehow, all we've suffered and all we will suffer is worth it, when you say that. Please, ask Him to take over in this situation, and give us both the strength to let each other go. He died for us so that we wouldn't have to live in the hell of our own thoughts and wants. *He'll make it all right, Precious.* Somday we'll look back on this awful day and thank Him for it."

They walked hand-in-hand to a nearby park bench, sitting down very close together. Jim put his arm around Marion as he prayed incoherently, and Marion buried her sobs in his shoulder. Soon she prayed too; then they both knew they could stand no more.

They stumbled back to their cars, saying little. When the final moment came, Jim squeezed her hand in his and blurted out, "Where will you go? What will you do? I know you can't go on with Larry just as if nothing had happened. You're so frail. It's too much for you."

"I'm going home for a few weeks," Marion said slowly. "Mother called last night. Daddy's ill, and it's perfectly natural for me to go. The break will give me the chance to get from God what it takes to go on with Larry."

"It'll do more than that," Jim said suddenly, his voice hardening. "It'll give me time to clear this place for good. There's a transfer in the wind for me and I'm going to take it. I could never stand staying around here where you are. When you come back I'll be gone."

The weeks with her folks were not easy for Marion. Her father's heart condition made it imperative that he have as little stress as possible. She had to force herself to be cheerful when her soul was screaming for help. As much as she dreaded seeing Larry again, it was almost with relief that she boarded the plane to go back west after two months; the thought of being in Spokane without having Jim was unendurable.

But how could she face the drab, meaningless days—with nothing to look forward to but the endless round of monotony with Larry? She remembered that C. S. Lewis once called the persevering of an unhappy marriage the "exquisite torment." Suddenly Marion felt prostituted and trapped.

One morning, walking through her kitchen, Marion felt she could take it no more. Suddenly a Bible verse came to her: "It is I; be not afraid." She remembered that these were the words of the Lord Jesus when He came to His disciples in the middle of a storm on the Sea of Galilee. He had calmed the storm after He walked on the water toward them. Somehow His words to her then let her know that He would calm the storm in her heart as well.

She decided she had to tell Larry about her affair with Jim. He was stunned and broken by the news, but said very little. His loyalty to her amazed her. For the first time in years, the couple began to pray together and have family devotions with their children.

Some days were so dark that Marion wanted to die. One day, two other verses came to her, attended by great peace. "Satan has demanded permission to sift you like wheat; but I have prayed for you, that your faith may not fail; and you, when once you have turned again, strengthen your brothers."

Before long Marion noticed that people were coming to her with their problems. To her amazement, many were involved in crises like her former one, and desperate for answers. She began to have a love for others which was totally new to her life.

Sometimes she would say very little to the ones that came. She found she could rejoice with those who rejoiced, and weep with those who wept. The Lord seemed to be opening up old channels within her spirit which had been clogged by self-ishness and self-pity. His love flowed through her life, at last. It was not a strained, effort-borne thing, but a serene current of compassion.

The great test came two years after Jim and Marion parted. One day, without warning, they found themselves facing each other in the San Francisco airport. All the color drained from Marion's face, and her knees trembled terribly as Jim spoke to her.

During the next few moments, Jim spilled out his story. It was sordid and self-centered. After he left Spokane, he had become involved in a full-fledged extra-marital affair. Now two families were seething in the boiling pot of suburban slander.

Marion was glad when her flight number was called. As she boarded the near-empty plane for home, she was thankful that she could sit alone with her thoughts. Every trace of delusion she had long nurtured about Jim was gone; this man she had just spoken with was only a shell of the man she had once loved.

Why, Lord, he was never worth it! He never gave

up anything, did he? He just gave in—to his own passion and selfishness. Never mind the repercussions to his family. He doesn't care how much they are suffering because of him. Why, he didn't even seem to want to hear about me or what I've been through. He just didn't care! How could I ever have wasted so much love on him?

When Larry met her at the airport, the first thing Marion noticed was the way his tired face lit up at the sight of her. As they rode home together, she told him what had happened earlier in the day.

"Thank you for being so good to me," she whispered in conclusion. "Please forgive me for not appreciating you so many times."

"That's all right, Dear," Larry said. "No matter what we've been through, I'd still rather be married to you than some predictable bore. I've missed you, Marion. It's great to have you home—like sunshine after rain."

"Larry," Marion said slowly, "do you think I could have been wrong about what marriage is all about? I mean, do you think it's a place to grow up in?"

"Sure," Larry said easily, "and don't forget, most of us start as kids in the beginning. Trials speed up the process, that's all."

"I guess trials are like rocks on a steep mountain path, aren't they, Honey?" Marion added in wonder. "You've got to climb over them if you're ever going to get to the top; but sometimes you think you won't make it when the going is rough. But praise Jesus! He is with us no matter how steep the climb."

CHAPTER SIX

WALKING BY FAITH

Late one Sunday night in a comfortable mid-
western parsonage, a strange battle was
fought and won. A dynamic but disheveled young
pastor lay sprawled on the library floor in the
moonlight, his forehead propped on his elbows, the
fingers of both hands clenching hunks of his hair
as he stared at the rug. His wife and children had
been asleep for hours, and the church next door
was dark. Little did any of his well-to-do parish-
ioners dream of what he was going through (or
his family either, for that matter).

Just a few hours earlier he had told his congregation that he planned to resign and step out
into a faith ministry. He had smiled confidently as

he said, "Where God guides, He provides." He had sensed the presence and power of God upon him as he watched the shining faces of his wife and six daughters sharing his moment of abandon to the mercy and grace of God. He had laughingly reassured his people as they filed out, many of them expressing concern that the Stevens' family needs would be met in this new venture.

Dave had been so sure of the Lord through it all. Throughout the whole day, he had sensed an anointing beyond that which he usually experienced, and a deep consciousness of the Lord's presence. But where was his God now? Suddenly he was aware of suggestive thoughts, prophesying his doom. With stabbing accusations, the unwelcome phrases plunged through his mind.

You fool! Now you've really gone and done it! Cut off the branch behind you and there you are —some spectacle, on the cut-off piece! So you think you're going to blame this foolishness on God, do you? How about when you make a complete failure of it all, and have to come crawling back, begging your denomination to give you some spot somewhere? How will you feel then? What kind of glory will God get out of that? Suppose they won't take you back? Why did you have to leave the denomination anyway? What are you, some kind of fanatic? How do you think you'll feel when your daughters are hungry, and come beg-

*ging to you for a decent meal? How will Sally like
cooking oatmeal three times a day? You fool!*

"Oh, God, help me!" Dave moaned. The Lord
had never seemed so far away. The doubts rushed
in full force.

*Why not call the chairman of your Board right
away and tell him the whole thing was a gigantic
mistake? It's not too late to change things. Everyone makes a mistake now and then. You were
overwrought, that's all. You're tired. You've been
traveling too much, preaching too many other
places. Delusions of grandeur. Your people like
you. Go on, swallow your pride and go back.*

Suddenly a Scripture verse came to Dave's mind
as the sweat poured from his forehead. "No one,
after putting his hand to the plow, and looking
back, is fit for the kingdom of God." [1]

Then another part of a verse flashed through
his mind: ". . . the accuser of our brethren has
been thrown down, who accuses them before our
God day and night." [2]

Dave jumped up and paced the study floor.
"Why, of course! The accuser! It's Satan who's behind all of this. You get going, Satan, in Jesus'
name—you hear me?" Dave spoke right out loud.

As if a light had been turned on, everything now
seemed different. The shadows in the moonlit

[1] Luke 9:62.
[2] Revelation 12:10.

97

study seemed friendly now. The macabre atmosphere of doom vanished, and with it, Dave's own "all-is-lost" feeling. He could smile again. He flicked on the light switch of the high-intensity lamp on his desk and pulled out his Bible. Opening the fly leaf, he wrote out Matthew 6:33. "Seek first His kingdom and His righteousness, and all these things will be added to you." Then, afterward, he added these words: "I believe God," and signed his name, with the date.

The first testing the Stevens had to face was the matter of housing. With a large family, they had need for a big place, but big places cost money. Daily they lifted this matter to the Lord, and daily they had His peace that He had heard them and would not fail them. Time passed quickly. Soon there were just five days left before Dave's pastorate would end. That night a phone call came in from a Christian friend about to move to another city, who did not want to sell his house. Would Dave, Sally, and the children like to use it for a nominal rent? It was more than adequate, with five bedrooms and two baths. The amazed couple assured their friend that they would be delighted to use it as long as it was available, and moved in the day after the other family left.

A part-time job which required Dave's attention only three mornings a week proved to be the

Lord's provision for the basic needs of rent and utilities during the first few months of their new life of faith. Gifts began coming in from strange and surprising sources, which put food on the table and kept the car running. Invitations to speak in other areas were more frequent, which meant that Dave was traveling much of the time. Best of all, evenings and afternoons at home could be devoted to the literature ministry which Dave felt was more and more God's will for his life.

The book and pamphlet distribution center began in the unused half of the Stevens' two-car garage. Soon it mushroomed into half of the basement, and finally one of the girls gave up her room and moved in with her younger sister to make more space available. Right after this happened, it became obvious to Dave that time was now as big a problem as space had been. He gave up his part-time job, trusting that God would meet their need for rent money in another way.

Confident that the Lord would send in a big check or two just to cover the rent by the time it was due, Dave and Sally trusted and waited. The night before the rent was due, Dave and Sally fasted and spent two hours on their knees seeking God for His provision. Just after supper, the telephone rang. It was a long-distance call from their landlord.

"Hi, Dave!" Al said.

"Hello there, Al," Dave answered reluctantly, dreading what he had to tell him.

"Say Dave, Nancy and I have been talking about our house arrangement, and we're just not happy about it. We've been praying about the matter all this month, and we're sure we've got the Lord's answer."

"Oh? What is it?" Dave could hear the tension in his own voice, and the pounding of his heart. How could they ever pay more rent *now*, when they didn't even have what was due?

"Dave, we just don't feel right about charging you and Sally rent. We know God will provide for all of our needs; in fact, He's given us a lot more since we've been helping you in the small way of giving you low-rent housing. Now we're excited to see how He'll work when you folks put all that you have into your ministry and meeting the other needs of the family."

"Al, do you mean that? Are you sure you might not be sorry real soon?"

The light on Dave's face let Sally know that the answer had come, although she couldn't imagine how. Her eyes filled up with big, happy tears.

"Of course I mean it, Dave. I'm sure you have other places to put the money from that part-time job."

"Well, as a matter of fact, Al, I've quit that job. We've found that the Lord's giving us too much to do to fit anything else in. And I've got to be honest with you. I had no money to send you tomorrow, and I was wondering how on earth I was going to break the news to you."

There was a long, low whistle at the end of the wire.

"Wow, Dave, I'm glad you told me that. It's been a real urgent thing this month. We couldn't put off praying about it and making up our minds *now*. That was God, all right! Suppose we hadn't obeyed?"

"The big point is, you *did* obey, Al. We've really been finding out that this life of faith is 'living in the midst of a miracle on the edge of disaster.' But the great thing is that *God always comes through*."

"Yeah," Al agreed in real wonder. "He sure does. Thanks for letting us be part of the miracle. Our love to the whole gang."

As Dave hung up the phone, and hugged Sally, he remembered the Lord's words to Peter when the apostle was walking on the water. He had taken his eyes off Jesus, and started to sink. Jesus said to him, "O you of little faith, why did you doubt?" [8] And in that quiet moment, Dave knew that the same strong Hand had reached out to him.

The next big trial Dave and Sally faced was the bad news that their old car, which had done

[8] Matthew 14:31.

101

125,000 miles, would do no more—not without at least three hundred dollars worth of repairs. There was no money for the repairs, nor any way to get another car. It was very, very black that afternoon as the Stevens prayed, although the sun was shining outside.

Again, the phone rang.

"Dave?" Bob Zimmer asked.

"Yup, right here," Dave answered.

"Listen, the Lord has really been blessing my wife and me in our car-leasing business since we went into it. In fact, we're doing so well right now we'd like to say 'thank you' to Him in some way. We've been praying about it, and we've decided we'd like to let you folks have a new station wagon every year to use, just like it was leased. Only there'll be no charge."

"Praise the Lord!" Dave exploded. "Bob, you don't know how timely this is! You see, our old car just died, and we sure didn't see how we were going bring a new one to birth."

"Say, that's great, Dave!" Bob sounded exultant on the other end of the wire. "Now we can cut down on the volume of the 'journey mercies' prayers as you do all this traveling. It really bothered us, you going far and wide like you've been in that heap."

Several years have passed since the car episode,

and the Stevens have had many other opportunities to trust God. He has never failed them.

Recently, while Dave was ministering to a very poor congregation on a weekend and knew the offering would be small, he felt led of God not to accept any money from them. When the treasurer approached him with a check for $125, he was amazed. Immediately the Lord reminded him of his decision.

"Thanks a lot, Mr. Andrews, but I can't take that. The Lord's shown me that this money is needed right here."

The treasurer's eyes bulged, and his mouth dropped open in amazement.

"Do you really mean that, Mr. Stevens?"

"Sure I mean it." Dave was beginning to feel uncomfortable. The spectre of two large bills he knew were due began to loom up in his mind. One was a fuel bill for $74.60. The other hadn't come in yet.

The treasurer grabbed Dave's arms with his two big, swarthy hands.

"Mr. Stevens, you're a prince. We had a bad leak in the church this past week, and the plumber had to come or we couldn't have had these meetings. His bill was $125, and I can tell you frankly, I just didn't know how we were going to pay."

"Well, praise the Lord! I know that feeling!"

Dave said, as a real warm glow came over him. "Matthew 6:33 is still in the Book!"

When he got home, Dave dreaded to face Sally with what he had done. Predictably, the other bill had come. She showed him the little slip of paper with the matter-of-fact figure written on it— $49.35. Dave winced as he did some mental arithmetic, and began to open his own mail which had come in his absence.

The first letter he read was from a well-to-do friend of his, who was also a lay preacher.

Dear Dave:

This will be short, for I've got to catch a plane home in a few minutes. The two groups I just spoke to insisted on giving me an honorarium, but these things just present a tax problem to me. I'm endorsing both of them over to you, with the thought that we might make this a steady arrangement. When these come, just take them from the Lord as if they were gifts for your own speaking engagements.

In the faithful God,
Chuck

Dave looked at the two checks in his left hand. One was for fifty dollars and the other was for seventy-five.

"Sally," Dave said, as he looked up at his wife, "did you know our God *always* comes through?"

The Stevens have faced one big temptation in the life of faith, which to many of us would seem to be a provision. About a year ago, an elderly widow called them and asked them to come see her. When they got there, she informed them that she planned to leave them her home when she died.

For the next few weeks, both Dave and Sally prayed about this possibility. They had recently helped a new mission in the inner city get off to a start, and they knew the Lord wanted them to continue to live nearby. Their present home was just a twenty-minute drive from the mission, but the widow's home was two hours away. Gradually they became convinced that the house should be sold at her death and the money given to the mission. They suggested this to the widow, and found her overjoyed at the prospect, a real confirmation of God's will.

Recently, my husband and I spent an evening with the Stevens, and asked them to sum up for us how they feel about this life of faith. Dave said he'd have to think about it for a few days.

A short time later we received a tape in the mail. The following are his comments on that tape.

"In retrospect, I have no doubts about the decision to step out on faith. I now have perfect freedom to preach the whole truth in a way that my congregation never really wanted. It was extremely difficult to keep from either offending them or offending the Lord. When I knew I had to make the decision, I figured it would be much better in the long run not to offend the Lord. Of course, the Bible teaches that; but it's a lot easier to read it and tell others about it than it is to do it. Living the words of the Bible, denying self and carrying the cross—that's the tough part.

"Because I did give up the security, I'm able now to preach the things that have been revealed to me openly and without apology. In going through all this, I've received a considerable education about the provisions of God. I've learned more in this short time than I had before in my lifetime.

"I used to find it extremely difficult to preach to people about the total commitment of their financial resources, when I wasn't committing anything. I had it made.

"We've discovered that God does supply our needs, but not necessarily our wants. The security blanket of the pastorate was really weighing me down, and I didn't realize it. Now we're living dangerously, and it's really exhilarating; it's a great experience. But like all experiences of this nature, the reality of it can never be felt until the step of faith has been taken.

"If you had told me four years ago that I would ever do such a thing, I would have laughed you out of the room. At that time, the thought of giving up a steady income, with six children to support, would just have been unheard of.

"I've had a great release in my life as a result of being away from the influence of those church members who are not Christians. It's so easy for a pastor to try to please everybody, including the unbelievers. But so often when you try to please the unbelievers, you end up displeasing God. Now, as long as I'm attempting to be faithful to Jesus, if I don't please somebody, it doesn't bother me. There may seem to be times when nobody *but* Jesus is pleased, but that's better than displeasing Him.

"Now, here's Sally. She has a few things to say."

The lilting, cheerful voice of this active, pretty mother of six, whom I enjoy as a real friend, came as a perfect conclusion to the thoughtful, soft-spoken comments of her husband.

"The feeling I have is one of freedom—especially the freedom to do God's will. We're not concerned about pleasing people, but pleasing God; that's our ultimate goal.

"We've had plenty of opportunity to find out if God really means it when He says not to worry about clothing and food and shelter for tomorrow —and He surely does supply all our needs—from a house, right down to a book rack. The joy of serving the Lord in the way in which He directs is tremendous. Having to look at Him continually for guidance puts us in our proper place. (It's very deflating to the ego, believe me!) Our faith and obedience to Him are always being tested. We've had to give up worrying about what we would do for money if the washing machine broke down, or one of the kids got hurt, or the offering was small.

"If the Lord has kept the universe running this long, our small difficulties should be no problem for Him at all. Our daily lives are so exciting, because we are actually seeing and experiencing God at work. He works in such delightful and surprising ways that life with Him is always new —or in the words of Jesus, *abundant*."

CHAPTER SEVEN

C.T. AND 'SCILLA

In our busy, modern life, few people take the time to read great missionary biographies. Yet these are rich with thrilling testimony to the faithfulness of God toward those who withhold nothing from Him in seeking His best. This concluding testimony represents the very summit of Moriah climbing.

Few men have laid more on the altar than the great missionary pioneer, C. T. Studd. Once a wealthy, internationally famous cricket player of the Cambridge and all-England Elevens, Studd turned his back on worldly achievement to sail for China with the Cambridge Seven in 1885. All outstanding Cambridge University graduates, these young men became missionaries under the China Inland Mission, wore native dress, and lived and ate as the nationals did among whom they worked.

After two years in China, the twenty-five-year-old Studd became convinced that he should give his inherited fortune to the Lord. Like Abraham, he obeyed immediately, and sent away his "Ishmael" into the care and keeping of God. One of the checks he wrote out for the Lord's work in India arrived at the Salvation Army headquarters just after they had spent a night in prayer for reinforcements. With this thrilling and generous provision, a party of fifty new workers was sent out.

Soon afterward, C. T. met a sparkling young girl from Ireland who had just arrived in China. Once Studd had said that if he ever married, it would have to be a "Salvation Army Hallelujah Lassie." Priscilla Stewart was just that. When God has great souls who have turned their backs on everything in life but Him, He can entrust them with a great love and know they will burn out together for Him. These are the great love stories of all time.

At first, when C. T. proposed, Priscilla refused him, apparently because she was determined to be in the will of God, and as yet had no assurance about marriage plans. Excerpts from his letters to her during this period speak for themselves:

"You have neither the mind of God nor the will of God in the matter, but I have. And I intend to marry you whether you will or not, so you had better make up your mind and accept the situation. . . . but here I do say that after eight days spent alone in prayer and fasting, I do believe the Lord has shown me that your determination is wrong and will not stand, and that you yourself will see this presently, if the Lord has not shown you already. . . . Day after day passes and I only get more and more convinced about it, and I cannot doubt it is of the Lord, for you know somewhat of how I have spent the time since receiving your letter: everything else has been laid aside, occupation, sleep and food, and I have sought His face and to know His will, and He has led me straight forward, and day by day He speaks to me and gives me encouragement and emboldens me to ask definitely for you." [1]

In one letter, sixty-eight pages long, and written while C. T. was recuperating from a major illness he says, "It will be no easy life, no life of ease which I would offer you, but one of toil and hardship; in fact, if I did not know you to be a woman of God, I would not dream of asking you. It is to be a fellow-soldier in His Army. It is to live a life of faith in God, a fighting life, remembering that here we have no abiding city, no certain dwelling-place, but only a home eternal in the Father's House above. Such would be the life: may the Lord alone guide you." [2]

Four months later, after Priscilla had agreed to marry him, C. T. wrote these amazing words: "Now before I go further, I just want to beseech

[1] Norman Grubb, *C. T. Studd*, p. 84.
[2] Norman Grubb, *C. T. Studd*, p. 85.

you, Darling, that we may both make the same request every day to our Father, that we give each other up to Jesus every single day of our lives to be separated or not just as He please, *that neither of us may ever make an idol of the other*."

This Moriah-prayer was put into the form of a vow at the actual wedding ceremony of these two chosen vessels of God, which took place after each of them had suffered near-fatal illnesses. As Priscilla and C. T. Studd knelt together and made the traditional vows, they also promised God, "We will never hinder one another from serving Thee."

For ten years the Studds labored for the Lord together in China, but rapidly deteriorating health forced them to return home with their four little girls in 1894. Soon afterwards they were to know their first extended period of separation, when C. T. traveled extensively in the United States for the Student Volunteer Movement. During his eighteen months here, many young people's lives were committed to Christ and ignited by the power of the Holy Spirit.

From 1900 to 1906 the missionary family served the Lord in Ootacamund, South India, and Mrs. Studd wrote home during this time that every week, two or three people found the Lord through their witness. Their own four girls each came to a

8 Ibid., p. 85, italics added.

personal knowledge of Christ during the happy years in India, and were baptized by their father.

Two years after the return of the Studd family to England, this time for the sake of their girls' education, C. T. received the great call of his life. Through Dr. Karl Kumm, he was profoundedly moved by the plight of tribes in the unevangelized central portion of Africa who had never once heard of Jesus Christ.

Neither Studd nor his wife had good health at this time, and medical reports of the doctors who examined him were so negative that no board would sponsor him in his determination to go to Africa. In fact, even his greatest admirers and friends made it clear to him that they regarded any attempt of his to travel to Africa as suicidal. However, as he waited on God, C. T. felt more and more sure that the Lord would have him go —alone. Thus he sailed, in December 1910, bound for Khartoum.

After many months of trekking in Africa, and the discovery of vast areas where no missionary had gone before, Studd returned to England and shared his vision with people everywhere. It was during this period that he wrote several stirring appeals which were used of God to call many men into His service. He also made direct platform appeals. As in his earlier days, Studd found the college students responding to him most readily, and one student joined him in 1913, when he left on his great trip to establish a work in the heart of Africa.

The night before they left, another young man sat up late talking with them. As the immensity of Studd's sacrifice began to dawn on him, he said, "Is it a fact that at fifty-two you mean to leave your country, your home, your wife and your children?"

"What?" said C. T. "Have you been talking of the sacrifice of the Lord Jesus Christ tonight? If Jesus Christ be God and died for me, then no sacrifice can be too great for me to make for him." [4]

These words, spoken from the very summit of Moriah experience, were to become the motto of the Heart of Africa Mission—and later the World-wide Evangelization Crusade—which Studd founded. The man of God never waivered from this conviction, nor attempted to take back what he had laid on the altar for God's sake.

He wrote to his wife en route: "Well, my Darling, God was good to keep us so busy that last night. He knew I could not stand much, and so He engineered us right through and gave the glory in our souls. I shall ever picture you running up with the camera. I longed, but dared not, say good-bye or kiss again. I dared not. . . . You little dream of how I know that you paid the greatest price,

[4] Norman Grubb, C. T. Studd, p. 141.

only I did not dare say so to you, but I do admire you, Darling, and shall ever do so, and God will give you His hundredfold." [5]

"Mrs. Studd was a semi-invalid, having to spend part of each day in her bed with an enlarged heart. Shortly after her husband's departure, he wrote back to tell her of his miraculous recovery when seemingly near death through fever, and said to her, 'Now 'Scilla, you trust Dr. Jesus also and get up off your bed.' She did, even with a return of her trouble, and as undaunted as her husband, became a flaming challenger to youth to go out and join her husband, and took on the home operation of the mission, sending out thousands of pamphlets, writing twenty to thirty letters a day, and editing the early issue of the *Heart of Africa Mission Magazine*." [6]

Studd saw England only once more in his lifetime, two years later, when he came home to encourage others to join him in the work. He saw his beloved wife only once more after that, many years later. In 1928, just a year before she died, she flew to visit him for two weeks. Norman Grubb has captured the feeling of that last encounter between husband and wife in his description, which follows:

"Some 2,000 native Christians gathered to meet

[5] Ibid., p. 142.
[6] Letter from Norman Grubb, 3-10-71.

her. They had always been told that their Bwana's wife was at home, so busy getting white men and women to come out and tell them about Jesus that she could not come herself; but when they saw her in the flesh and realized that there really was such a person as 'Mama Bwana,' they then began to understand, in a way that no words could bring home, the price that Bwana and his wife had paid to bring salvation to them. From that time onward, some of the Christians saw in a new way what it cost Christ to redeem them, and what manner of men they must be in the light of such sacrifice. . . . They said farewell to each other in his bamboo house, knowing that it was the last time that they would meet on earth. They came out together from the house and down the path to the waiting motor car. Not another word was said. She seemed completely oblivious of the group of missionaries standing round the car to say good-bye, but got in with set face and eyes looking straight in front of her, and was driven off." [7]

That was in 1928. A year later, Priscilla Studd was called Home to be with her Lord. In 1931, shortly before his own death, C. T. Studd wrote this analysis of his life, as part of a letter home:

"As I believe I am now nearing my departure from this world, I have but a few things to rejoice in; they are these:

[7] Norman Grubb, *C. T. Studd*, pp. 235, 236.

"1. That God called me to China and I went in spite of utmost opposition from all my loved ones.

"2. That I joyfully acted as Christ told that rich young man to act.

"3. That I deliberately at the call of God, went alone on the Bibby liner in 1910, gave up my life for this work, which was to be henceforth not for the Sudan only, but for the whole unevangelized world.

"My only joys therefore are that when God has given me a work to do, I have not refused to do it." [8]

One can surely hear the divine commentary on such a life echoing over the years: *"Because you have done this thing, and have not withheld . . . indeed I will greatly bless you, and I will greatly multiply your descendants as the stars of the heavens . . . and in your descendants all the nations of the earth shall be blessed; because you have obeyed my voice."* [9]

It is wonderful to see how literally the Faithful God keeps His promises to such a follower in Abraham's footsteps. Only forty years have passed since C. T. Studd went home to Glory, but God has already fulfilled His Word to His servant in many ways. C. T.'s son-in-law, Norman Grubb, is

[8] Norman Grubb, *C. T. Studd,* p. 239.
[9] Genesis 22:16-18.

now director of the mission Studd founded, and has graciously summarized the record of God's faithfulness as follows:

"The Worldwide Evangelization Crusade which he first founded as the Heart of Africa Mission has now extended to forty fields in all corners of the earth. In place of the blackness of that first field of the Congo, which he named 'The Devil's Den,' there are now some 700 churches under their own leadership, numbering some 40,000 members. In the other forty fields, such as in Colombia, South America, in the islands of Java and Sumatra in Indonesia, in nine West African Republics, in India and Pakistan, tens of thousands have turned to the Lord and are being built up in their local churches. The Christian Literature Crusade came into being in 1941, and now has 100 bookcenters in 35 fields, reaching out further by many bookmobiles. All told there are 12,000 workers in the two crusades, not counting the dozens of national workers, and with the training centers in Britain and Australia continually filled.

"It is fifty-five years since C. T. Studd opened his first mission center in Niangara, the geographical center of Africa, which he built for $40 and called 'Buckingham Palace.' Through these years God has sent millions of dollars to these Crusades without the necessity of a single appeal to man, sufficient for all needs of the work—food, buildings by the dozens, automobiles, traveling expenses, and all supplies for the missionary families —exactly as He told his servant who gave up all he had for the spread of the Gospel, who preferred to trust in the Bank of Heaven, and God's promise in Matthew 6:33. All praise to, Him." [10]

[10] Letter from Norman Grubb, 3-4-71.

EPILOGUE

As we have "climbed" together through these pages, perhaps you have sensed a vague unrest in your spirit. There is a throne in each of our hearts where either Christ or some usurper sits. It is a very private place, but no matter how cleverly we keep it hidden from the eyes of men, God sees who reigns there.

Stephen Olford once said, "Either Christ is Lord of all, or He is not Lord at all." Do you want to make Jesus absolute *Lord* of your life? If so, here are a few thoughts that may help you to avoid certain pitfalls on the way.

First of all, you will be tempted to lay your "all" on the altar. Now, I have never seen an "all" and

I doubt if you have, either. Years ago when my husband and I were studying at Columbia Bible College in preparation for missionary service, Dr. G. Allen Fleece said that we like to stay in the realm of generalities, but God deals with specifics. We would prefer to put our "all" on the altar, but God says put *this thing* or *that one* there. He always puts His fingers on the one thing that most stands between us, and He is very sticky on this point. He cannot be distracted or convinced otherwise, no matter what our arguments.

Second, you may be subtly influenced to *procrastinate* in your decision to yield to God's will. After all, are you not weak, battered, and buffeted at the moment? Will it not be better to wait until you go to some conference, or have some crisis experience, before you face your Moriah? The answer to this question is an unequivocal 'no.' We have an enemy whose business it is to see that the multitudes in the valley of decision stay there— without ever deciding. Just as "now is the day of salvation," so is now the day of decision, for you know not what a day may bring forth. The Bible says that our life is as a vapor, that appears for a little time, and then vanishes away.[1]

Third, you may be looking at others you know, and comforting yourself that you have about the same commitment to Christ as they. Why become

[1] James 4:14

a fanatic? The answer to that question is simple. Because you won't stand before Him on the basis of their standards, *but His,* that's why. "So then each one of us shall give an account of himself to God." [2] "He that rejects Me, and does not receive my sayings, has one who judges him: *the word* I spoke is what will judge him at the last day." [3]

Remember, the Lord Jesus Christ said that. *"Lord"* means He is boss; what He says goes. There is no court of appeal or reference beyond Him. *"Jesus"* means "Jehovah saves." The one who is Judge is also the Savior; He has come down off the bench and taken all of the penalty for sin which He has imposed and which we so richly deserve. *"Christ"* means the chosen one, the anointed one. No one else will do.

How can yoú say "no" to *Him?*

Remember—Abraham got up early in the morning and did it. Round up your young men; cut your wood for the fire; sharpen your knife. Bring your Isaac out of hiding, and set out for the hill country.

Climb Mount Moriah!

[2] Romans 14:12.
[3] John 12:48.

Suggested Inspirational
Paperback Books

THE ACTS OF THE GREEN APPLES
by Jean Stone Willans $1.45
Once upon a time, the Willanses were quiet, respectable suburbanites. The story of how they got to Hong Kong is the heart-warming miracle-studded and frankly hilarious account of *The Acts of the Green Apples*.

FACE UP WITH A MIRACLE
by Don Basham $1.25
This is a fascinating book about God the Holy Spirit bringing a new dimension into the lives of twentieth-century Christians. It is filled with experiences that testify to a God of miracles being unleashed in our lives right now.

FAITH UNDER FIRE
by Chris Panos 95¢
Learn the secrets of fiery faith, as Chris Panos shares with you the insights that have enabled him to heal the sick, win thousands of souls to Christ, and smuggle Bibles into Iron and Bamboo Curtain countries at the risk of his life.

GILLIES' GUIDE TO HOME PRAYER MEETINGS
by George and Harriet Gillies $1.25
He is a retired Wall Street executive. She is his wife. Together, they wrote *A Scriptural Outline of the Baptism in the Holy Spirit*. Now the Gillies bring us this practical, step-by-step handbook dealing with the problems and procedures involved in setting up the kind of home fellowship that will bless the lives of all attending.

HOW GREAT I WAS!
by Doug Foley $1.25
Doug Foley was a young, ambitious engineer who woke up one morning to find all his dreams shattered by the words of a neurologist who told him, "You've got disseminated sclerosis." *How Great I Was* is the gripping true story of the miracles that brought Doug Foley back to health in spirit, mind, and body.

HE SPOKE AND I WAS STRENGTHENED
by Dick Mills $1.25
An easy-to-read devotional of 52 prophetic scripturally-based messages directed to the businessman, the perfectionist, the bereaved, the lonely, the ambitious and many more.

IF I CAN, YOU CAN
by Betty Lee Esses $2.25
The wife of charismatic teacher Michael Esses tells how Jesus saved her husband and her marriage and shares what He's been teaching the Esses ever since. For Betty, these were hard-won spiritual insights. For you, they can come easy; all you have to do is read this book.

IF YOU SEE LENNIE
by Char Potterbaum $1.45
Char Potterbaum was so full of pills her husband claimed she rattled when she turned over in bed. Learn why she doesn't need pills anymore—and how she exchanged her depression for joy—in a book that combines everyday, homespun humor with true spiritual wisdom.

KICKED OUT OF THE KINGDOM
by Charles Trombley $1.25
It all began with a totally unexpected *miracle*—healing of his baby daughter's clubbed feet. Trombley's Jehovah's Witness friends said, "The devil did it!" But Trombley asked, "Would the devil do anything as beautiful as this?" From beginning to end, this is the story of God's sovereign move in the life of a man who really wanted to know the truth.

LET GO!
by Fenelon   95¢
Jesus promised a life full of joy and peace. Why then are so many Christians struggling to attain the qualities that Christ said belonged to the child of God? Fenelon speaks firmly—but lovingly—to those whose lives have been an uphill battle. Don't miss this one.

A MANUAL ON EXORCISM
by H. A. Maxwell Whyte $1.25
The Exorcist posed the question; this book has the answers. Are there really such things as demons? How can you know if you have one? Can anybody cast out demons? These and many more troublesome questions are clearly answered in this helpful book.

THE NEW WINE IS BETTER
by Robert Thom $1.45
Anyone with problems (and who hasn't got problems?) needs to read this story of one man who saw the invisible, believed the incredible, and received the impossible. A

lively and often amusing account of Robert Thom's downward trek from a 12 bedroom mansion in South Africa to the hopeless world of an alcoholic on the verge of suicide —and the whole new world of faith and power Robert Thom discovered after Mrs. Webster came knocking on his door.

PLEASE MAKE ME CRY
by Cookie Rodriguez $1.45
The first female dope addict to "kick the habit" in Dave Wilkerson's ministry, Cookie was so hard people said even death didn't want her. Told the way it really happened, this is the true story of how Cookie found Someone she wanted even more than heroin.

THE PURPLE PIG AND OTHER MIRACLES
by Dick Eastman $1.45
Hidden away in a rambling, wood-frame house on "O" Street in Sacramento, there is a special underground room where Bible-believing Christians pray twenty-four hours a day, seven days a week. Miracles? They happen all the time. And the prayer power is spreading . . .

THE RAPTURE BOOK
by Doug Chatham $1.25
Almost everybody seems agreed that old planet Earth is a time-bomb about to go off, but here's a different slant—a slant which is backed up by the age-old prophecies of the Bible. Exciting teaching about the next event on the prophetic calendar!

SCANDALOUS SAINT
by John C. Hagee $1.25
It all started at the tender age of 4, when John Eiles got his picture in the newspapers a notoriously young "culprit." From that time on, he was into one hair-raising scrape after another. Arrested for using a sound truck, jailed for smuggling contraband into Mexico, charged with using his church as a house of prostitution his story proves that a saint's life isn't necessarily dull!

SEVEN SPLENDID MOMENTS
by Carmen Benson $1.25
Plain days and dragging hours can come alive with beauty and splendor—if you know the secret. We think you'll find the secret in this book, a collection of intimate and true short stories designed to acquaint you with God's perfect Truth.

SIMMER DOWN, SAINT
by Jody Woerner
$1.25

Anxious? Uptight? Lost your cool? Simmer down—and learn how to add health, strength, peace and joy to your everyday living as the author shares with you a series of insights designed to steer you away from the wrong turns and potholes scattered along the straight and narrow way.

THE SPIRIT-LED FAMILY
by Grace Robley and
Wendell (Rob) Robley, M.D.
$1.25

Family life doesn't have to be a contest, pitting one member's interests against another's. If your family life isn't all you want it to be, this book will show you how you, too, can experience the love, peace, joy which is meant to be yours.